Read Me

Speak Me

Ann Enenbach

Ann Enenbach books are available for order through Ingram Press Catalogues

Ann Enenbach

Visit my website at www.readmespeakme.com

Printed in the United States of America

First Printing: March 2015

Published by Sojourn Publishing, LLC

ISBN: 978-1-62747-092-6

Ebook ISBN: 978-1-62747-093-3

To my parents who taught me to love my life. To my family and friends, who showed great patience, kindness and love, as I was writing my book.

Contents

It all began so cunningly and would change my world forever. After the sudden death of my husband, writing became my daily obsession. I recited my love poems aloud, convinced he could hear me. The hours I spent writing each day became the best of the twenty-four when I could sleep no more.

As time progressed I turned to more cheerful, even humorous, subjects. Because my writing became so prolific, I questioned the value of it. I decided to take a writing class to improve my skills. My professor became my first mentor. A writers' club invitation appeared and some good suggestions and comments came from my colleagues. Taking their advice, serious poetry was to become the order of the day. Articles of current events and short stories followed. Suddenly, I was at ease.

Eventually, a large body of work was finished. "What now?" I asked. Others around me were encouraging me to seek publication. After taking their advice I am at the crossroads of another new life. Remaining positive, I wait for my critics to settle my fate.

What Is Poetry?

"By poetry we mean the art of employing words in such a manner as to produce an illusion on the imagination; the art of doing by means of words, what the painter does by means of colors."

—Macaulay

"Poets utter great and wise things which they do not themselves understand."

—Plato

"Poetry is the music of thought, conveyed to us in the music of language."

—Chatfield

"Poetry is the utterance of deep and heartfelt truth. The true poet is very near the oracle."

—E. H. Chapin

"Poetry is the record of the best and happiest moments of the best minds."

—Shelley

"Poetry is the music of the soul."

—Voltaire

"Great poetry is that which stands the test of experience."

—Albert Einstein

"The poet is the rock of defense for human nature."

—William Wordsworth

"Poetry makes me feel as if the top of my head were taken off."

—Emily Dickinson

"Poetry is a series of explanations of life."

—Carl Sandberg

"Poetry. It is not the assertion of truth, but the making of that truth more fully real to us."

—T. S. Eliot

I Greet You Any Day

I am the silent beauty in your heart and soul.

The tiny place in the secret garden of your mind.

I will help you grow.

Never at rest.

Always creative.

I may sadden you.

Then cheer you.

I can put your thoughts into deepest places.

I will comfort you.

I'll make you smile.

All the while,

I am yours alone if you desire me.

Read me.

Speak me.

I am a poem.

Reality

We are what we want the world to see.

Never the pure reality can we be.

Those who say they are real,

is it just for appeal?

What's real or not,

I quite forgot.

Whatever you do,

you must be true

when the world

sees you.

Smiles

Smiles are so contagious,

Really not outrageous.

Crinkle up,

Don't wrinkle up.

You shall see

Your smile is

Like a mirror.

They smile right back,

Those folks you see.

Smiles are really

Meant to be.

Time

It slips away into a quickness.

I feel there is no way to grab onto it and hug it,

A bit savage-like.

Why is it, in my last years of life, I cling to time?

I never imagined I would.

Each moment captured, needs to be used in meaningful tasks.

Not too many days left, so hurry! Hurry!

No, hurry is not for me.

I will take the rest of my days patiently.

Hesitation

I wait.

I hesitate

To begin to do

The things I must do.

Why the pause

Whatever the cause?

Procrastinate... no.

I need a shove—onward, forward.

The task is at hand.

Why can't I be in command?

No more delays

I must begin today.

The rewards are great

For those who do not hesitate.

Persuasion

Listen to me.

What I am saying could be true.

I want your mind to hear my mind.

How can I know you will listen to me?

Persuasion is an art.

One mind joins the other and there you have "The Start."

A Decision

To make a decision takes vision.

Never complicate your thoughts

and the decision will come freely, easily.

Decide to open a door,

something is waiting for you.

How will you choose?

Once your decision is made,

complications will soon

begin to fade...

A Thought

"Someone has to worry," Mother would say.

It might as well be me.

Women worry about everything.

If there isn't anything to worry about then they invent something.

To quote, "Someone has to worry."

If worry would cure, we would have something fantastic here.

We wouldn't have events, situations, or irritating people causing worry.

Worry free; that's me!

Well, let's see, when would the worry start or stop?

Or, the reason to worry?

Someone else will have to decide that.

Organize the cure.

I can't be bothered, too much to do.

Everyone depends on me.

I rearrange my schedule to coordinate with theirs.

I am at their command.

Oh, now I am not worrying.

I am doing what I usually have to do.

I believe you must never worry about me worrying.

I am cured.

Guilt

The whys live deep,

deep in your mind.

It's impossible to sleep.

No mercy,

this guilt.

It repeats and repeats,

this guilt.

Never to forgive,

this guilt.

However, you must

surrender to forgiveness.

Forgive your own

tormented heart.

It's a start!

Olé

Having a little mirth

can get you a little girth.

Life's funny that way!

Enjoy, enjoy, for tomorrow you pay.

Weren't you king or queen for the day?

Olé!

Television Home Shopping

A jewel is to wear.

It sparkles, it sizzles.

And the price is right.

A merchant's delight.

A glamorous sight.

How can we refuse?

What's to lose?

It dazzles our neckline.

Razzle, dazzles our ears.

It's jewelry, no tomfoolery.

Why worry?

No hurry?

The selling is all American!

No payments until next year.

No fear!

Go right ahead: buy it, my dear!

Heaven's Door

It's a heavy door.

Takes a good life to open it all the way.

We will have our say

to the one who wears the crown.

Seems he has written it all down.

He wears a grin.

Oh my!

Looks like I'm in!

Just Laugh

Just to have laughed today

made it a wonderful, magical day.

It would have been an ordinary day

had we never laughed.

So, open your mouth, not to shout,

but to laugh at life and all its demands.

The world will hear your laughter

and it will echo back.

Another Day

It's a reprieve.

One more day to achieve.

Another chance for us

to glance at what we have found.

"Treasures abound,"

that's what I've found.

Now go and say

I'm profound.

The Meeting

What a treat when old friends meet.

When did time fade?

Seems only a glimmer.

Memories of play, school days,

or where and when!

True friends were a gift,

one to the other.

Building memories always was time well spent.

It didn't have to be a special event.

Well, true friends, let's remember the past

and forever make it last.

The Same As Equals

To be a self-made man

is an often heard remark,

an observation.

Do we hear the self-made woman,

often or ever?

What a compliment

to come easily to a man.

A woman

who has struggled through,

seems long awaiting the same praise.

Let's give a cheer

for those women who fought the same fight.

They deserve equal acclaim.

Onward, fellow men and women,

forever the same as equals.

Oh, Wondrous Dream

Will I ever be my pure imaginary 'she'?
On an elephant with a sequined blanket under me
deep in far off Afri-Kee?
Sailing to Bali,
am I able?
Japanese temples calling me.
Skiing down Mt. Blanc
and seeing Chamonix below.
Looking fabulous on Rio sand.
The Parthenon lighted
just for Ann.

London mist and Paris lights.
Have to take it slow.
My very own seat
in the Coliseum in Rome.
I pause no more to roam.
All this magic that lets me be 'she.'
My dream ends.
My heart sings.
Oh! Wondrous dream!

Post Script

Having done some pretty serious traveling in my years, this was fun to write! A spoof on travel by my imaginary "she." The imaginary "she" has brought me fun but also a bit of trouble from time to time!

Chapter One Dream

Dreamed of my life on another planet.

Things so delicious I begged to be true.

To taste peace, to forget time.

Future thoughts untouched.

Space and time far away.

Can't I stay?

Earth stands quietly by.

Return to my own place, I hesitate.

Mother says, "If it's too good to be true, walk away."

And so, I obey.

Day and Night

I never wanted to be alone

when darkness became light.

When sunbeams awaken me

dreams are now in sight.

I know what life expects of me

and God has planned as well.

A day to be well lived, I see enables me.

When evening stars are in the sky

my work is now complete.

Toss my worries in a heap

when I require sleep.

Night has fallen once again

and I am now at peace

to sleep.

The Internet

The internet doesn't have me yet!

Is it ignorant bliss, this wonder of the world I missed?

I wrote a letter today, in my usual way,

with beautiful stationary and pen in hand.

I was in complete command.

No text, no email, no tweets

no eyes locked to a screen.

I managed to communicate sight unseen.

When my letter arrives, it will be a surprise!

"The gift of the pen and of the pad!"

Yes, a beautiful handwritten letter is about to be had.

Ah, the Good Life!

Life is not for the weak, the meek,

or those afraid to speak.

Doesn't society with its huge ego

say how we must live our days?

We search for those to emulate.

Are they there, somewhere?

Searching but not finding

can be a brutal fate.

Trust and belief in yourself is a

tonic not to be denied.

A life worth living is a life dedicated to

finding the sweet contentment

and peace within ourselves.

We deserve it.

Ah, the good life!

Bother Me

Wait!

Don't go away!

Bother me.

Attention me.

Compliment me.

Conversation me.

Listen to me.

Desire me.

Romance with me.

Dance with me.

Have fun with me.

Live life with me.

Don't set me free!

Please, oh please,

Bother me!

Music and Lyrics at the Cocktail Party

Music fills the room.

Martinis flow to those

in the know.

Glasses, bell-like,

twinkle and touch.

Wishes too good to be true

help the cocktail crowd

from feeling blue.

Music and chatter are endless.

The crowd is captivated

for the night.

Escape is near for one.

Everything was background music to him.

He slips quietly into

the night.

The Man

The President spoke again

today in his "usual positive way."

In our world, actions

speak louder than words.

We hope he can keep

his many promises

Made to us in his

"usual positive way."

The list of his dreams

is long.

We pray he is strong.

Is he up to the task?

Well, what more can we

hopeful Americans ask?

In our own

"not-so-positive way."

Enthusiastic You

Whatever you do,

try to have some enthusiasm

to see it through.

It is not easy to do.

Complete your goals.

A journey not to be denied.

Along the path

seek harmony and savor life.

Have a slice.

Go ahead.

Take a big bite.

It's quite all right!

Good Thoughts

Use them wisely.

They fade behind a cloud,

so catch them quickly.

Keep them tender,

before you frown.

Dark corners of the mind

are better left behind.

Good Thoughts,

you have permission

to own my mind.

Whatever Life Serves You

The banquet of the day is our gift to savor, enrich you.

Walk the path of life slowly.

Do not measure time, or time will measure you!

Do not choose your weapons.

Just sing your way to the Door of Heaven.

Moving into the New House

Boxes, boxes everywhere.

Do we care?

Tempers flare

just regarding placement of a chair!

Placement of furniture

makes a house a home,

So I've been told!

Boxes, boxes everywhere.

Really, do we care?

Sweet happiness and contentment

is what we seek in this

new house and

everywhere.

The Wave

The wave with a life of its own

rushes and caresses his body.

The pounding of its thunder

echoes the wild pounding

of his heart.

Waves surround him,

engulfing him.

At last, The Thrill,

only the Divine could send,

begins for him.

A pure cascade of

water cleanses him.

Splendid moments are his alone.

He now owns the

Magic of the Wave.

Post Script

This was written for my grandson Andrew, an ardent surfer. You can see Andrew early in the morning riding the waves he learned to love at age four in Newport Beach, California.

Oh! The English

The British, I say, so well beloved
in their manicured ways.
They are charming and often
most alarming.
Their high tea, their cold
and dashing sea.
On an island they live,
no other quite like it.
Dramatic, uncanny,
their broad, startling accent
takes you away,
I must say!
I want to be in their countryside
and be lazily alive!
These gracious people,
no others like them.
I guess I'll enjoy them.
I will listen to their roaring sea
and please don't bother me
while I am in Britain.
I am entirely smitten.
"Yes, dear girl," they beckon to me.
Wishing to be British
is surely, just me!

Cry a Little

Not too much

A baby fountain

A tiny bunch

A wail, a moan

A little sigh

Builds our tears

into a cry

New Cry

It's all right to cry

The angels cry—

The heavens, too!

Never question the why

They all cry

So why not I?

The Rain

I love the rain.

It cleanses me, caresses me!

I want to splish-splash

my sandaled feet in it.

No umbrella will I need.

Thunder cracking, lightning

with its full dramatic show.

I love it so!

Rain must have the scent of itself

falling on lilac trees in Paris,

on that rainy day in May!

The promise of emerald green—to last.

Can it leave a rainbow

at little children's feet?

Oh, so sweet!

Yes, yes, let it rain.

Let it pour.

It's never too much

rain, for more!

My Guests

They have arrived!

Suddenly, I feel more alive!

One year gone!

It's been too long.

Sweet lullabies I hear

When my family appears.

I want to cry!

But why?

I will shed, no, not one tear,

For they are here!

Four-Letter-Word Society

A language lost, but oh! the cost!

The dictionary is not in sight.

Descriptions are prescriptions for disaster.

Doesn't seem to matter

to those who abuse.

We have fear that

all is lost to the sweet

vocabulary of words!

Let's leave the four letter words

to those in disgrace.

Post Script

I'm concerned about the prevalence of swear words, etc., on TV and in the movies. The human race amazes me!

The Convertible

With the top down,

a hat to soften the wind, I begin.

It's not just a drive

it's about being alive!

It's a journey from the

ordinary to the extraordinary!

What a ride!

The ocean is beside.

It's me feeling free.

So alive

in my dream car ride!

Oh yeah! Even at eighty-five!

A Favorite Birthday Wish
To Whom It May Concern
"Happy Birthday"

On the day that you were born

the clouds tucked themselves away.

The sun was at its sunniest.

The stars twinkled just for you.

The moon was dazzled by your birth.

The sky turned from lavender blue to a

star-studded navy blue.

You see

the heavens knew that

a star had been born.

Now we know it, too.

Twisted Nighttime

Night is twisted.

Sleep escapes me.

Wide awake, body aches.

Dream of sleeping.

Will I begin to weep?

Weep for rest so

I can face the world's harsh ways!

Devil moon says,

"If you live through the night you are a survivor."

Daylight comes and I remember

"His forty days and forty nights"!

Escape to Somewhere

My own distant voice is unable to speak!

No signal at the crossroads,

I hesitate!

Running in haste.

Directions are unclear.

My escape to somewhere is about to disappear,

In fear.

Contentment whispers,

"You are peaceful right here.

Your acceptance has no fear."

Around You

Lately, I just want to be around you!

I love your aroundness!

Wish to be, on restless days,

your Silent Sound.

When I am around you

I am at ease.

Wish to please.

So for now,

can't I just hang,

hang around,

around you?

Silence Speaks

Listen to your inner voice.

It's telling you what not to fear.

Sounds keep coming to an educated ear.

What it is saying,

its wisdom will unfold.

You only have to listen

to hear and then be told.

To Survive and Stay Alive

If I walked into the ocean

would it be some kind of potion?

To die or not to die!

What happens when you take your own life?

Those who stay will feel,

what did I do to save this soul?

I cannot sleep for all the strife.

She sent up warnings.

No one was listening.

She told them she cried.

Wanted not to survive.

Now she weeps in her far and distant sleep.

Her sleep for keeps.

Greatness

There are those tiny crevices in the mind that can

pave the way for greatness.

Greatness could be said about us, perhaps, one day!

It's not just for a Winston Churchill or an Emily
Dickinson.

We could claim it as part of our own destiny.

Greatness may be there.

Who can say?

Do we really want it?

Maybe not today.

The Antique Store

When I see the old, not the new,

why do I feel a bit sad?

The past brings thoughts and feelings.

It's just an antique store.

Items to explore.

Perhaps acquire?

Should I purchase what I have owned before?

The Melancholy Me declines.

Memories fade.

I depart hastily from

The Antique Store.

A View of Life

Sometimes with gladness,

there is a bit of sadness.

We cannot always be full of glee.

"It's all right not to be"—

Shakespeare said that to me!

It's perfectly clear, that

we are what we want the world to see.

The Unknown

There is a tunnel that I fear.

Just walk right in and disappear!

I'm waiting by a garden gate.

Will I hear someone say, "Don't hesitate"?

Well, I'm not ill

So where's the will?

I cannot walk that way.

Not today, I say.

To Accept a Life

The baby was born at dawn today.

Heaven's door opened and life began.

A life, so sacred no one could spare it!

The Creator's wish is:

"Accept this life; say a prayer."

The Newborn

Their bodies shared.

Souls were theirs alone.

She kept the body and

the Soul complete and warm.

A burden, or an act of love?

Nine months nurtured,

then the birth began.

The babe with its own Soul

left the body shared.

Its own body and Soul to keep.

An act of love.

Oh! So sweet!

Cry Baby Cry

The first cry of a newborn baby

into the world is a cry

Like no other!

To imagine his feelings

is to be a brilliant sage.

Perhaps, it's one of release,

to feel and to move comfortably!

His lungs expanding

for the first time

show his strength

to try and succeed.

A strong brave cry for

freedom—to live, to learn,

conquer life.

Yes, that first cry

will follow him for the rest

of his very own life.

A Happening

We were having dinner and she said, "My son would have been fourteen years old today. He died in infancy. I wonder what he would be like today if he walked toward me?" In answer to her, I wrote this poem.

A Mother's Reflection
"Never to Forget"

You remember the short life of a boy.

A darling boy, who still lives in your very heart and soul.

You wonder, would he be the tall lad you see in your dreams if he walked toward you today?

Will he be what you have imagined?

He will be anything, any fantasy that you have.

God sends these thoughts to comfort you.

Your son lives in Everlasting Life and Peace, not so very far away from you.

On this day of bittersweet memories, the angels in Heaven send you a message.

They say, "If you are thinking and loving him today, he is feeling the very same way."

Post Script

Ana is the mother who lost the son. I wrote this poem on August 12th which was both Ana's son's birthday and my late husband's birthday. Same day, same feeling, same sadness, same memories. I believe our lives touch one another in many ways, more often than we know.

The Soul

The soul is not meant to be seen.

it's somewhere in between

what we know and do not know.

It has its own life.

Understanding will forever be the mystery never to unfold.

We hear, "I am the way."

Then we realize what we must do.

What a marvelous goal

to save one's soul.

Darkness Came to Call

He had smiled and said,

"See you soon."

Now, the messenger was

rushing her to his side.

"We tried, but failed to save him."

Her heart was pounding

loudly against the silence of the deadly scene.

Sudden Death had come calling that day.

Don't Leave Me Alone

Come, enter this house where I grieve.

Please, do not leave.

Sleep comes at last when I hear moving feet.

Conversations, even laughter, it really doesn't matter.

I long for chatter!

You are with me in my darkest hours.

Please do not leave!

You make it possible for me to grieve.

Post Script

These few poems, written after my husband's death, are about wanting so much not to be alone.

Any Day, Any Weather

Twenty years later

and nothing but you

will do!

Listening to music today,

I know you loved also,

causes me to remember.

Melodies we both loved

seem to join spirits from above.

Is it true or just my love of the same music

that joins me to you when I feel blue?

Post Script

It is often said, and I believe that it's true, we must speak often of loved ones who have died. If we do not speak of them, it's as if they never lived.

More

Open a door.

Ask for more.

Is more waiting for you?

Do you possess enough?

Do I need more?

Think, I'll wait.

Not ask for more.

It's good to

close the door on more.

The USA at Stake

Politicians on a roll.

Selling us their very soul.

Will they keep their promises?

Weary people in our land

wish for a miracle.

These men, so human, yet

Superstars on view!

Do you suppose they really

could restore and then renew?

Listening to the vows of

those who wish to lead.

Do I believe?

My Country under a Cloud

All over the land

things are not good,

not right.

There is a strangeness here.

A bundle of worries

wrapped too tightly.

Not wanting to open it,

causes us to do nothing.

A cloud is over us.

What is it?

It's unrest.

Our country has failed to do its best.

I love my country; I just

hope my country still loves me!

Mothers

Mothers have that special touch

to teach their children

oh so much!

Children who always

seem to ask for more.

Nowhere to resign

from being a Mother,

You really wouldn't

want it to be any other way.

You can't ignore them

so just adore them.

Discipline

It should be the order of the day.

It imposes a skill.

Its behavior is in

accord with rules.

It sets the practice of order.

Words from Webster's ring true.

The real measure is up to you.

Plan and follow through!

Rules of conduct are hard to beat.

Regulations, discipline

must be the order of the day.

Post Script

I have known those with orderly minds. More to the point, discipline seems to be their good fortune. Discipline saves time and energy and leads to a simpler approach to daily life.

A Poem for St. Patrick's Day

It's a day for the Irish!

And the Want-to-Be-Irish!

Time to think green.

Imagine Emerald Horizons.

The Jewels of Ireland.

This land, this isle with its

people, history, folklore, music,

dance, poetry, all waiting for the

world to capture and love.

Visiting there, perhaps it's raining!

Better to perceive how green

the land will always be.

Land and sea, Ireland is

to love endlessly.

So, just be Irish for a little while.

You will see your winning

Irish eyes begin to smile!

Post Script

This poem was written in memory of my mother, Regina Murphy. She was 100-percent Irish and loved this holiday. Her father was Robert E. Murphy, all Irish. Her mother was Alice McCarten, also all Irish. It's always been a favorite in our family. The day you cook and eat Irish foods. Corned beef and cabbage and potatoes colcannon—so delicious. We always wore something green. "The Top of the Day": that was St. Patrick's Day to us.

Music

Music speaks to us

No matter the style.

It makes your heart beat softer

even for a little while.

Come dance, it says.

Listen to lyrics with a poetic touch.

Music, it's everywhere.

It's the bride's first dance.

It's the lullabies to put children to sleep.

A baton is lifted to it in a concert hall.

It's a Broadway chorus.

It's a singer's delight.

It's a trio's sweet jazz.

It's pure razzmatazz.

It's Rogers and Astaire.

It ain't goin' anywhere.

It's the carolers at your door on Christmas Eve.

It's any Cole Porter melody.

It's Gershwin at his best.

It's the wedding march.

It's the graduation walk.

It's the organ at the great cathedral.

It's the samba from Brazil.

It's the tango from Buenos Aires.

It's the hum of monks in Tibet.

It's Pavarotti at the Met.

It's a melody from Bach.

It's the skater's waltz.

It's Willie Nelson's country songs.

It's Sinatra crooning "Fly Me to the Moon."

It's the band on July Fourth in the big parade.

It's Preservation Hall where jazz is king.

It's the birthday cake song.

It's the big band at the dance on Saturday night.

It can be the love song favorite of your life.

Worries fade when it serenades.

It can be elegant.

It can be simple.

You can sit, stand, work, sing, or dance to it.

Yes, music.

Mighty fine music.

It's the music of your soul.

It can even be rock and roll.

It's haunting!

It's gorgeous!

It's a gift to the ear.

Well now,

You only have to listen to hear!

Post Script

Music is the most amazing therapy today. It is used in so many areas: medicine, schools, churches, hospitals, and retirement homes. So many places to heal and restore. Don't you even love it all the more?

An Open House

There was an Open House today.

An open heart feels little happiness this day.

Walls filled with memories are still.

"No one will ever love this house the way she did,"

her heart will say.

Lovely home.

Echoes fade.

How can she leave?

She cannot grieve.

The almighty dollar rules her fate.

No one sees her fears or dries her tears.

Yes, there was an Open House today.

Soft Tears on a Soft Windy Day

As time fades, I know for certain that you are gone!

Gone, but where?

Do you breathe the same air wherever you are?

There?

Where is there?

Truth, so bitter!

Memory is blocked by the real, never the false.

On this day of soft wind,

I look for you everywhere.

Viewing the sea and mountain

and, as I possess the day,

nothing replaces you!

Where or when do you imagine we will meet again?

I whisper aloud

The soft wind has no answer for me!

Post Script

Not every day is melancholy! Today was.

Rainy Day

Where is his face?

That face I cannot erase,

Somewhere in the heavens or far out in space.

It rained today.

Rained in every way.

My tears were raining, too,

I felt blue thinking of you.

Was it raining where you are,

and did you feel blue, too?

Cloud Puffs

Through the window of the aircraft,

on a flight recently, my imagination took hold.

Lavender blue skies and frothy clouds

were quite beautiful!

Everyone who loves clouds,

I wished for them to see this.

What are these cloud puffs?

Are they waiting to be snow slowly

cascading to earth?

Or could they be the frosting

on a birthday cake that hasn't

found the party place?

Could they, looking closely,

each and every one, be a secret place

for those we love and lost?

Do they dwell eternally in these

secret places and does heaven protect them?

Will we, could we, find these deep

hiding places some day?

Perhaps our loved ones will

show us the way!

Looking at these enormous formations

of incredible beauty,

I am peaceful, amazingly!

Settling back I had no idea

why my imagination had been so vivid.

Now, I felt the aircraft beginning

to descend and a sadness came over me.

A feeling that I was losing touch

with all those loved ones!

Being in these clouds,

having them fascinate me,

then suddenly looking up at them,

I knew that feeling would haunt me.

As I felt the aircraft come closer to landing,

reality became finality.

Had I truly imagined all of this?

Yes, it was final—the journey, the dream,

whatever it had been was that!

The finality was real, just as death is so final, I recalled.

I felt a chill come over me as I departed

the flight never to be forgotten!

Me

I am just me.

Not the girl I used to be.

This is all you see of me.

The Me who cannot see beyond the

Sea of Life.

It was, you know,

the very best of life.

There I go, the old, old wife

who had the husband,

Oh, so grand!

Who had six children

so polite.

That is what is me!

When Did I Grow Old?

I see the playground from the car.

Can I swing and merry-go-round from afar?

When did I grow old?

My inner voice, so young,

melted time, can I rewind?

Loved all my days.

When did I grow old?

Was it just today

watching children play?

Precious time I spent with mine.

Reflecting back, perhaps

I never have grown old!

Time never conquered me.

When I Am Gone

When I am gone sing no sad songs for me.

I'll breathe myself into a cloud and write poetry there.

A tiny star will light my pen and pad

so, don't be sad!

My spirit will enfold me.

Happy Me, I will be.

The Quality of Life

The quality of life

never easy to find.

Isn't it given to someone

by the Divine?

Work and play

always the demanding world's challenge

each day.

Givers and takers

always compete.

Shall we envy the elite?

Searching and not finding

can be a cruel fate.

The pure quality of life

seems worth the pursuit.

What is life really

without a goal?

That discovery can

enrich and nourish

even our own soul!

Quality of Life must reflect

purity of the Divine.

Everything and Nothing

We play a game in life.

"Too Much."

"Too Little."

Think it wise not to

want for everything,

better will be the game.

Nothing is the leveler

that makes us all the same

Listen to All the Young People

Listen to all the young people.

They want to be heard.

What they say

may hold you in dismay!

These young people want to

be free of worries,

not to hurry.

Conquer life in their own way.

"Our future seems so far away," they say,

"Be patient, your faith and trust will guide us

to our own self-esteem."

It's their journey

not to be denied.

Listen.

Their young voices are saying,

"We want to show the world

what we really can do."

Post Script

"Can do" is my phrase for success. I love it. It's great to remember—can do!

Clean the Screen

We all seem to like cleanliness.

Why is it hard to ignore the insults of the mind

and vision we are forced to watch?

It's TV time in our favorite place,

our home, our space.

Our home, our sanctuary,

not so sacred anymore!

We watch many indignities.

It soils our mind.

The children so young,

losing innocence in their special place.

It's up to us to change the atmosphere.

Entertainment not so tainted.

We are all to blame.

What a shame!

The Quake

No one speaks about the Quake!

It seems as if it could not happen here.

The "Big One"? no not here!

The long love affair with California is endless.

Everything is perfection!

The weather, beaches, California cuisine, great clothes!

Streets are named after flowers.

Beauty at all hours.

No, no earthquake will happen here!

People love California.

In this land of movie creativity and

make believe, it's easy to ignore the Quake.

California's image should never be at stake.

After all, this is "The Golden Sunshine State."

So now, please pardon me while I return to my

beautiful ocean view!

Oh, yes, my margarita, too!

Post Script

As time goes by it appears we have more to fear than the
Quake. It's the fires that we have to contend with and all

the damage and loss. We had always feared the Quake, but now there are fires. Californians are strong and can rise to face the problem. So, you see, we are not just a pretty place or pretty face. We are California at its best in times of stress.

The New House

Walls too wide!

Ceilings too high.

Something is just not right.

Where is the warmth?

Haven't even seen a mouse.

Furniture not placed.

Windows are bare.

Can we find comfort and happiness there?

Is this new house waiting to be loved?

Let's begin now.

Beds made linen sweet,

table set with familiar china,

so neat!

It's a beginning to love this house!

Light a fire.

Prepare a meal.

It's lovely, warm and real.

Can we begin to forget the past?

All these touches make this our

very own home, at last!

Pause

The Chinese say,

"Come have some tea with me and speak of absurdities."

How wise, they surmise!

The pause to cause a moment and speak of fun and of sun.

It's good for you and for me to pause and have a lovely cup of tea.

Post Script

This is not a Chinese proverb. It is my own composition following my trips to China and Japan. They do have great knowledge and know how to relax! When they use the term "absurdities," they mean just that: do not relax too seriously!

A Whirly Bird

A humming bird zipped by my window.

His little wings a humming.

Really wants to play,

the California way!

Quick, quick.

Gone in a blink.

These tiny birds,

more clever than we think!

Back to School

The lap of luxury is back to school,

where children rule.

Their teachers are in dismay!

When did all the discipline go away?

Homes not demanding enough.

Why not call their bluff?

You teach respect at home.

School is for learning,

not discerning.

Teachers won't fall into that trap,

so...

they are sending your children

right back to your lap.

A Family Affair

A family affair, why do we care?

Can they be a family united?

No, not they!

Relationships are in decay.

Order of place is in disgrace.

Grandparents, mothers, fathers, sons, and daughters,

grandchildren never friends.

Their view of life never to blend.

There is another family so different.

Action, love, and effort bless their clan.

Happiness is always in their plan.

Each family member plays a part.

Can the family who have lost heart,

begin a new start?

Don't close the relationship gate.

It's a wonderful event

When family affairs are sincerely content.

Imagination

There is no better life than one filled with imagination!

To form a picture in your mind is a fanciful delight.

"It's not true; it's only a fantasy," we hear.

The world of entertainment and art thrive on it.

It's powerful, magnetic.

We all love imagination.

No better life escape.

It challenges the senses.

Whatever you perceive,

Perhaps you may believe!

Post Script

Imagination is wonderful. It's a distraction when you need it. Children are natural with it. Don't we all love to slip away into the wonderful world—to imagine, to dream!

The Gem of the Mind

When I am in a faraway place,

I need to be curious about the place.

Never the ordinary, I explore, seeking more.

Another culture to discover,

adventures to uncover.

Curiosity: the gem of the mind,

I am ready for you to unfold

the next, best thrill of my lifetime.

I Never Tire of the Sea

I never tire of the sea.

I look and look, in wonder.

Then, suddenly, the sea looks back at me.

Its beauty never rests.

The tide with its vast waters will forever hug the shore.

Thunderous, roaring waves can even calm your restless ways.

We say once more, we never tire of the sea.

The sea has many faces.

Crystal waves become laced

with pastel colored splashes

on a sun filled day.

Crashing against the sea wall, the ocean

seemingly is applauding itself.

Convinced that the ocean is aware of its own beauty,

we watch endlessly.

A vast audience loves the ocean and all its many changes.

A rainy-day ocean can suddenly appear without warning.

When the storm begins, raindrops measure the ocean's horizon.

Waves scatter as a stormy sky is shouting,

thunder with a roar.

It's rain falling on the sea itself,

on the ocean floor.

Lightning bursts its very core.

The sun with all its powers

whispers to the rain.

The rain will listen to the sun.

The storm will settle and fade quietly away.

It will begin with the sun warming the sand and shore.

The power of these elements working together is fascinating.

Now we are feeling the sea calm once again.

Its simple message amazes those who care and love the ocean.

The message of peacefulness and contentment for all.

Its splendor once again showing us its power.

It knows, and we must know, too

this ocean, this sea,

will always be.

It's meant... to just be.

Post Script

I began my love of the sea and watching the ocean while living in Coronado Island, San Clemente, and Newport Beach. Whenever I moved, there was that fascinating sea with changes each day.

Sights and Sounds of Ocean Blue

It's a surprise

to see the sunset

dipping down to catch the waves

and set them all aglow

with golden splashes.

Now the ocean has its own sunset too.

It is a never ending painting,

to view all the contrasts and changing beauty at the seashore.

Post Script

When I see the reflection of the sun on the water, I believe it is the water's very own sunset. Imagination: the gem of the mind always working its charms. Well, for me, anyway!

Sunsets

Sunsets, they say,

are perfect endings to a perfect day.

What about the sad days and how they end?

Can sunsets comfort when misty tears

cloud the view?

Sunsets glow for everyone,

the happy or the sad!

That's what makes them unforgettable.

They are a gift from the inspiration of the Divine

for all mankind.

Post Script

Having written often about my love of the sea, I continue to feel peace and happiness while I am there. It inspires a writer every day.

Twilight Time

Twilight was painting

gold and muted colors

on a charcoal dark sky.

Today was drifting away.

The moon was capturing light

for its moonbeams to shine,

when night began to call.

The sun shed a tear,

not wanting to disappear.

Twilight Time had arrived!

The heavens were turning day into night.

What a glorious sight!

Enjoying this magical time,

the world seemed to be just fine.

The Insignificant Me

It doesn't matter whether

I ride the subway or bus!

Millions out there

simply do not care!

The world goes around and around

and I have no sound.

I am just

the Insignificant Me.

Carefree Thinking

Deep thinking can harm your inner self.

Question your goals.

Disturb your peace.

Too many demands come from deepest thoughts.

So scatter those fears,

relax those doubts.

That's what carefree thinking is really all about.

Look No More for the Me You Wish to See

The poem that follows is my version of what someone with Alzheimer's would say in their own voice.

Look no more for the me you wish to see.

In my deepest eye and ear,

nothing is quite clear.

So many are pleading.

Do you remember me?

Do you recall?

Who is she? Who is he?

"No," I reply, "not at all."

I see this day the way I live now.

Kindness and all,

it's their fear that I hear.

Well, I have no fear.

I ask you,

the woman that you think you know,

please, let her go.

Let me remember the sun.

Let me have fun.

Just let me be.

The me I am now.

Approval

Approval, I've heard

is a way to observe.

Are they looking at me?

What do they see?

A wink, a nod, applause from the crowd?

Whoever they be,

they always will be looking at me.

Post Script

Who are they anyway? We quote them so often and really don't know who they are. We treat them as critics and how foolish that is. Caring about too many people's opinions of us can take years away from freedom of being your own person. So few in this life really and truly think of you that often, let alone criticize you. So go on now, and do not be too hard on what life expects of you. I believe it expects too much of us in some cases. Be gentle with yourselves.

Love's Meaning

Love is beyond description.

There is never a prescription

to fill our hearts and souls with it.

It makes us smile, even for a little while.

It's here, it's there, everywhere,

for all to share.

It's the greatest gift of all

from the "He" who makes the call.

It's there for all.

To win, to lose, to choose.

This Life

Life is long and

full of littleness.

I want to love life.

Will life love me?

It's a blend of nice

and not so nice.

Let's put out the fire

with a little ice.

The Political You

Now the whole world is "political."

Ask a favor.

Return it back.

Know all the right people.

Scratch their back.

Who you know.

What you do.

Be the cunning

political you.

It's quite all right.

We all do!

A Dream Forgotten or Not

What is that dream we dreamed?

Not always serene, it's an illusion.

Can we capture it once more?

The mind speaks when it rests.

When the memory is so clear,

perhaps, we should listen.

Shall we live that dream again?

Reality will decide.

In the sheer mist of memory recalled,

shall we listen and hear?

The dream is only

remembered for what it was,

an illusion!

Best forgotten.

Reality speaks, always,

ever so clear.

Moment to Moment

Moment to moment.

What does that mean?

Is something happening

in between?

One moment is a measure of time untold.

Another moment can be

a thought to unfold.

Count moments together

to capture added hours.

Whatever the count,

it's all borrowed time.

It's all under the

watchful eye of the one

in control of their moments.

The "always Divine"!

The Beautiful Young

Every song should be

sung while you capture

the sun.

Age slips too quickly away!

The young have time.

Our days slip away in

timeless ways.

With the Beauty of Youth

energy thrives!

They are so alive!

We, as we grow older, say to them,

live and love "the Circle of Life"

with sheer delight.

You are the beautiful ones!

You are young!

Post Script

One of my children remarked, upon reading this poem, that older people too have wonderful qualities. I was not comparing the beauty of the young to the wisdom and beauty of the elderly. Not at all. It's just a view of what it is to be young. Is it wasted on them, as someone said? I think not.

Money

Money hides behind reality.

The amount is paramount.

It's a lesson for equality.

Those who have it

seem not to care.

Those without it

are in despair!

So what do we do?

Whatever our fate

money will always be

The Greatest Debate!

The Shoeless Grandma

There once was a grandma.

She lived in no shoe.

She did have so many grandchildren she didn't know what to do!

Their birthdays, Christmases, events galore kept coming.

She just can't do giftin' no more.

So, how can she tell them,

to be the best players and follow their dreams.

That she'll always love them no matter the year.

Their lives she holds dear.

Her best wishes she sends,

whatever the occasion,

whatever the year.

Post Script

So many people on fixed incomes are faced with buying and giving presents, especially those who have grand-children who are young and do not understand. For el-derly people, this can be a dilemma. A handwritten letter is a thought, one remarking on their accomplishments and talents. It might help with the older children, but perhaps not with the little. During the year I try to col-lect small gifts and put them aside. They are happy with any gift, I've learned. Perhaps they will remember the generous years gone by.

My Best

I have done my best!

I'll have my say.

Now, it's that time!

The sun sets here in the West—

The West I do so love!

Golden California heaps

its sun on me.

I could shed a tear

for all the loveliness here.

I never want to return

to where I once was, you see,

this is where my final days must be.

It's my one and only destiny.

Ageless Beauty

Can I be quiet and still

today or conquer the world

in my own calm way?

The game is gone but

"Life Goes On."

I am wise at last.

Oh, what a learning past.

I'm here to stay—

I am that ageless beauty.

Beauty of mind, heart, and soul

Not body or face!

I can conquer life now,

because Life has not conquered me.

Words

Words, the magic of them is so powerful. They seem to string the world together. Language changes from border to border. Communication continues through the transfer of language from country to country. Words open doors, most of all, our thoughts, hearts, and minds. We must use them wisely with great responsibility.

Words are what we

need to use constantly!

Brilliant language

to hear,

not a four-letter score!

It's such a bore!

The sweet vocabulary

of life is so uplifting.

Four-letter words bring you down to a level

of ignorance and poor taste.

They have no style!

In the end, no fun.

Boring, they become!

Beautiful words hug

your soul and keep

you special.

When you speak your best and finest,

you are what the divine

surely had in mind.

About the Author

Ann Enenbach is a widow who lives in Southern California. She has been writing for fifteen years and writes every day. She has composed short stories and commentaries but her first love is her original poetry. Ann has written many poems with this collection being her first and the finest she has to offer.

Ann has a zest for life and is a curious soul. She believes she can still conquer life because life has not conquered her. She has had careers in travel and interior design. Music and the arts are her favorite ways to relax. Music is so integral to her life that Ann can't imagine life without it. Her poem about music is one of her favorites.

Ann has six children, seventeen grandchildren, and six great grandchildren. She is currently writing a children's book.

Ann hopes to be remembered as being ageless while she traveled through her life.